About the Author

Andy spent most of his adult life working in business but, with a background in art and music, continued his creative output. Having to care for two young children, he lost his job and had time to develop his poetry and writing. Andy hails from Manchester, studied in Liverpool, then moved to Bristol where he lives. He loves the unique blend of being close to two vibrant cities (Bristol and Bath) and a rural environment all around to explore.

Heart Stones

Andy TS Cowell

Heart Stones

Olympia Publishers
London

www.olympiapublishers.com
OLYMPIA PAPERBACK EDITION

Copyright © Andy TS Cowell 2021

The right of Andy TS Cowell to be identified as author of
this work has been asserted in accordance with sections 77 and 78
of the Copyright, Designs and Patents Act 1988.

All Rights Reserved

No reproduction, copy or transmission of this publication
may be made without written permission.
No paragraph of this publication may be reproduced,
copied or transmitted save with the written permission of the
publisher, or in accordance with the provisions
of the Copyright Act 1956 (as amended).

Any person who commits any unauthorised act in relation to
this publication may be liable to criminal
prosecution and civil claims for damage.

A CIP catalogue record for this title is
available from the British Library.

ISBN: 978-1-78830-859-5

This is a work of fiction.
Names, characters, places and incidents originate from the writer's
imagination. Any resemblance to actual persons, living or dead, is
purely coincidental.

First Published in 2021

Olympia Publishers
Tallis House
2 Tallis Street
London
EC4Y 0AB

Printed in Great Britain

Dedication

For Olivia and Louis
In memory of Melanie
1966 to 2005

Acknowledgements

Thanks to Jane Reece, my mentor in building this collection and to everyone in the Memoirs Writing Group at The Folk House, Bristol; and the Poetry Group at Yate Library.

Contents

Take It as It Comes 15
    Take It as It Comes 17
One The End 19
    A Beautiful Mess 21
    She's Gone 22
    The Awful Truth 25
    What If Nothing 26
    We Cannot Know 27
Two Hello I love You 29
    Valentine 32
    Holiday 35
    A Well-Earned Break 36
    Listen 37
    Mummy's Wiggle 40
    Shall We Dance? 44
    Three Peaks 45
    Cold Feet 48
    Too Young 51
    Wallpaper 52
    Last Night 54
    First Day at School 56

Three Love me two times 57
   Leaving 59
   To Mum 61
   Heart Stones 63
   Best Friend 64
   Father's Hand (I) 65
   Rose 69
   When I Grow Up 70
   When I Was Three 72
   Did I Say Goodbye? 74

Four When the music's over 75
   Daft Dad 77
   Every Day 82
   Chop, Chop 84
   Father's Hand (II) 86
   Puddles 89
   Who Cares? 95
   Letters You Did Not Write 97
   Dad Day 101
   Waving? 103

Five People are Strange 105
   Kids Are Horrible Part 1 Ring O' Roses 107
   Kids Are Horrible Part 2 Playtime 108
   Kids Are Horrible Part 3 Time Heals 110
   The Gardener 111

Haiku 115
Extra Time 116
Hymn to Whoever 118
Be Kind 121
my good health 123
Why? 124
I Can't Say How You Should Feel 126
Hit the Ground Running 127
Six My eyes have seen you 129
  First Date 131
In Blood 135
Gardens 137
rearviewmirror 16/4 139
Let Go 140
Snowflake 141
Three Things You Should Know 142
How Far You've Come 143

Take It as It Comes

Take It as It Comes

Two perfect lives, one perfect team;
Children's lives full and content.
Fate's finger points and turns the dream
From Heaven to Hell sent.
To fall from such highs to the lowest of low;
A shock that is too hard to take.
With one parent lost, they learn how to grow,
While the Father, mistakes he does make.
Learning to live with grief from the loss,
The bonds much tighter become.
The dice they roll, the coins they toss:
One Father, one Daughter, one Son.
    Tribulations and troubles toil overcome,
    Their story is told yet not done.

One
The End

A Beautiful Mess

What a beautiful mess was left,
When from together we were cleft.
Taken in your prime, young lives in the shade;
Hopes shattered, future plans unmade.

What cruel endeavours destined us,
A higher hand struck without fuss.
I queried, "How could this be done?"
Innocents hollow with you now gone.

Turned upside down to start again,
No easy path. A troubled stain
That cannot be wiped away with ease.
Turn home and sleep on bended knees.

Close the doors, lock windows too,
"Tears augmenting morning dew."
Who do you weep for? Yourself denied.
In bed, the empty space beside.

She's Gone

As I drive away from that fuck-shit place,
my eyes look down from the road ahead at
the phone sat in its cradle just to the
left of the steering wheel. In the car, I
shouldn't do this; my emotions are high,
tears still falling onto my already
stained shirt. But I have hands-free, and I need
to tell someone.

"Mum. (deep breath)
It's Melanie. (silent pause)
She's gone."

These words I mutter slowly and mechanically
as if in a language just learned, and I
have to be sure to say it right, partly
because I am half watching the road and
partly because I am half in a daze.

There is a pause then a wail, a scream,
a sigh all mixed as one, but I don't hear it.

In my head I am singing:
"She's go-o-o-o-one oh oh I,
I'd better learn how to face it;
She's gone."

Hall and Oates are one of your favourite bands and this,
one of your favourite songs and now,
it plays between my ears;
the word 'gone' stretching out like a tape machine flutter.

RED LIGHT!!!

The Awful Truth

Now I have to look into their eyes
And tell the awful truth.
How to say it without some small lies?
A dagger to their hearts.

So young and small, with all ahead.
How can they understand
The shock of this loss? What will now be said?
This future never planned.

Their eyes. Their innocent eyes.

Their eyes stare back.
Like doll eyes that stare and scare,
Empty, unblinking. Nothing there.

I want to look away but must not.
Words stumble out, just a few.
How many does it take to say?
"Mum's never coming back,
Gone away."

What If Nothing

What if nothing ever happened?

No soft leather made for us to sit upon;
Glass carefully blown and shaped
Was never made.

Needles fashioned into the sharpest points
From metals heaved from rocks in the ground,
Did not form into something useful.

What if billions of years ago
Nothing collided.
And we never became,
Never bumped into each other.

Would that be better?

If I hadn't known you, would you live, love or die?

Would that be better?

We Cannot Know

We cannot know
What we do not know.
But if we did,
Would we change it?

Two
Hello I love You

Together we have made a home, a family, a wonderful life.
Together we have great strength.
Together we laugh and sometimes cry.
We can overcome anything, together....

I LOVE YOU

X X X X

Valentine

A smile as broad as sunshine
illuminates the room with a warmth
that puts us all at ease.
The fountain of happiness
that bursts forth from your lips,
as a daffodil in spring is invited
to open by the light you brought.
Your laughter: not gentle, resonates and reverberates
rolling infectiously around, caught
by all whose ears involuntarily receive it.
None can decline who come into your space.
Drawn without resistance;
your magnet pulls me closer.

"Hello."

You with your friend, I with mine
not supposed to be there.
It begins.
We begin a life-changing chance meeting
that takes us both to places
never gone before.
Longer for me, it still goes on.

I knew from that first laugh, the smile
in your voice, I would already love you.
The echo that bounces down the years
are two reminders that live on through you.

Through Us.

Holiday

The kids are packed, bucket and spade,
Towels and shorts, sandwiches made,
Car seats and belts, all buckled up
Ready to go without a stop.

That was the plan, to keep going
With food and drink; a song to sing.
But toilet breaks and "are we there yet?"
Slows down the time it takes to get

To our home, for a week by the sea.
On the beach where we can have tea,
Watching the kids, happy in play
Together. Our first holiday.

A Well-Earned Break

We decided for our first
Escape we would go to Italy.
Even in spring, it would be warm and dry, rain
Keeping away; we were certain.
Each destination we examined
Needed careful consideration.
Does it have places of interest to visit and

Is it easy to travel around?
Nearby, is there a beach or country walks,

Remote villages with real food?
Overall, for a few days away,
Might there be enough to do?
Everything reviewed, we made our decision.

Listen

We sit awhile and wait,
"He's late."
And wait alone.

"He's with another patient,
Be with you soon!!"

The door swings, open wide,
"Come on inside, sit down."

Two empty chairs bid,
Endure their upright position.
Two empty souls,
Hopeful.

One side of a table between
One voice.

Listen.

A still unsmiling face
Delivers the message.

"It's not good news, I'm afraid.
But we know what to do; we have a plan,
A course of action to take you through."

In one ear and out of the other;
His words a jumble of sound,
A meaningless wave pushing air through my drum
To my brain, that makes no sense of what it
Does not want to hear.

Listen.

Seated bodies still, eyes exchange glances from one
To the other, and the other.

We stand up, open the door to
The corridor of uncertainty,
The corridor of power,
The corridor that is a pathway unknown
In the hands of others now.

"What did he say, what did it mean,
Who do we tell now, what will we say?"

A confused jumble of sounds and words
Trying to define what we've been told and what we will do next.

Listen.

It's a long corridor, double doors at the end lead to another
And another.
Seemingly no way out.
Which way do we go,
And how will we know
If we are right?

Mummy's Wiggle

They told you the side effects of chemo,
So you knew it would happen.
Coming out in clumps in your hand
And hairbrush was still a shock.
Losing your eyebrows too, all your body hair;
It helped you, you said, with aqua dynamics in the pool.

Have a short cut first as the patches grow,
Not too drastic for when it's all gone.
That didn't last long. No creeping baldness.

I went for a Number One and picked the kids up from school.
The look on their faces as they walked down the path
To the gates
Where all the parents gather, all mums.
No one spoke to me at first,
Just a look of 'I know why you did that'
And then a 'Hi, how are you?'
A deadpan face.

The kids were not so obtuse.
They pointed and out loud, very loud, choked,
"Dad! What have you done?"

Answering their own question in unison,
"You've shaved your hair off!"
They laughed.

At the hospital, they had suggested a headscarf;
No way.
Or a wig.

Neatly lined up in a room to one side
(looked more like an old store cupboard to me)
Were polystyrene expressionless white heads
With a selection of hairpieces,
Not very carefully 'placed' on top.

You cried.
Not a loud outburst,
Not even much of a noise.
I saw your shoulders quiver
As you raised your hand to your eye
To wipe away a tear.

The nurse saw it too.
And the look she had seen many times before.
"Don't worry, we have some others
Or, if you choose one yourself from
A hairdresser or wig supplier (we have a list),
The NHS will contribute."

You tightened your lips with a sarcastic tilt
Of your head.
That made it *so* much better.

You found one, I won't say you liked,
That best suited and had it 'fitted.'
That's what they called it.
I watched them put it on your head and fiddle about
For a bit until you said, "That's okay."
I didn't disagree.

There you were, in the hall, when the kids came home
From school that day.
They called to you as I opened the door,
"Mum! Mum! Have you seen what Dad's done?"
They didn't seem to notice anything different about you,
Too busy dragging me to show you my bald head.
Even when you replied, "Yes, but look at me.
What do you think of MY hair?"

They looked at you, then me
Then back at you
Then me again.
Comparing these two opposites,
Reversals in elegance.

"Mummy's got a wiggle!" Louis blurted.

Awkward silence.

"Can I try it on?" He persisted,
Filling the gap.

Louis ran up and down the hall singing,
"Mummy's got a wiggle; I've got a wiggle"
Shaking his hips as he did so.
He ran to the big, tall cupboard at the end of the hall,
Took out a pair of gloves from the drawer,
Your big fur coat hung up
Then continued to run up and down,
Wearing a massive coat dragging along the floor
And oversized gloves that flapped about.

You laughed;
We laughed.

Shall We Dance?

Chair in the corner, comforting
Arms close up embrace
When settled in.

Wood burner flickers and glows
In the heart of the room,
Giving out heat and low light.

Half-full bottle of wine signals to be poured.
Italian blood red
That remembers warm Sorrento days.

In the background, soft entice from
Emmy-Lou's lips invite, "Here, There and Everywhere."

Shall we dance?

Three Peaks

We had been doing this for months, ten of us all kitted out in full walking gear, prepared for any weather or event. This day, it was warm, and as we left the miles behind us, so the layers fell off — like peeling an onion, each piece of clothing stuffed into the rucksack increasing its weight. They have to go with you. Though we would like to leave them in a hedge for later retrieval, they will be needed again to warm us, higher up above the treeline. It would be good to lose some weight though. Drinking the water helps, and no need to stop for a 'comfort break' — it all sweats out.

This was the third time we had been to Wales and the Brecon Beacons, so we know the way. Or so we thought! About two hours into the walk, we realised that the path looked somewhat familiar. "How the hell did that happen?" pipes up Haydn.

"What do you mean, H?" drills Ash. "You're the one with the map!"

"No! I gave it to Dave," H fires back.

H turns to Dave. "Dave".

"Where is he?" Chris calls from the front.

It would help to know that Dave has brought his dog with him again. A cute little Border Terrier called Polly. Our walk on this training session was measured to be about fifteen miles (more like twenty-five now we've gone wrong!) but I reckon that Polly would be doing three times that! While we all walk like squaddies, regimented on a straight-line yomp, Polly is all over the place — zig-zagging here and there, running on ahead in dog heaven, snout in the air or troughing the scrub, the scent of every creature living there up her nostrils.

Turning around, not only could we not see Dave, but we couldn't see Polly other. The terrain was up and down and fortunately, it didn't take long to backtrack to the previous dip and catch sight of Dave and Polly arguing (in that human versus dog kind of way) about which way to go. "Polly, Polly, come here, now, HERE!" protests Dave. One-sided you might say.

As we continued on, fitter now from our frequent training exercises, I took more notice of the landscape. I scanned the distance, my eyes wandering and wondering and, in my mind, a symphony, drifting back and forth, melody changing direction like the winds we faced.

Wales is a beautiful country. I love the south coast around St Davids. Here it is, bleak: moors, valleys, and peaks that sing to you, draw you in and take you away. We all need an escape, a door to open and take you into another place far from reality. The bad things. A corporeal abstraction into another land and, in my head, conceptual and fanciful. At that moment, I had both.

We sat in the pub after completing our accidentally extended walk, supping a welcome pint — some prefer ale, some cider. I'm a Northern beer drinker, unlike most of the rest of my West Country platoon. With a bunch of maps that Haydn brought, we discuss our final training mission before we tackle the real thing in a month's time: The Three Peaks.

Cold Feet

"My feet. My feet are cold," whispering as you slowly sink down
Into the pillows, your whole face a frown.
I peel back your socks. Your feet are blue,
A pale sky colour, a dull murky hue.

And the room is cold in a different way, a small side square off a much larger place;
No chatting and laughing and movement apace.
No.
In here, it's quiet, no windows or light,
No view of the gardens, the walls are all white.

Yet, at the same time, it's stuffy and hot,
A steam room, a sauna, so how is it not
Possible to have a warm body,
Warm feet?

Dozing now as I hold your hand, peaceful and slow
Forgotten what troubled, just moments ago.
And I start to think as the planet gets stuck;
The clock ticks stretching out
A fading beat.

I think about what it means, 'Cold feet'.

A strange saying really, to back down, retreat,
To give up on something you meant to complete.

Give up? A coward? Turn your back?
On something you started, there's something you lack.
Perspiration, Determination, Courage, and Strength.

Not You.

You never gave in or believed it would fail
So why is it all wrong?
To end with a whimper, having lived life with a bang,
Is a finish on its head that doesn't stand;

A soft bean bag that flops on the floor.

We heard it once, some months before,
Another in-patient.
"This hot-water bottle will keep your feet warm,
Or take a short hospital tour."

She seemed to take ages, and then she was here,
Helped up to her bed by a friend from her walk.
The children were playing, allowed into the ward
By the corner. Not hearing the talk.

I look back at You, now moved to this hole.
I can stand, and see,
Through the window down the aisle where the others all lie;
The soft breeze blowing blossom to the ground,
And listen to the silence of Your sound.

Too Young

Too young
To know what lies
Ahead, they sleep in peace.
We knew by then of course too well:
The end.

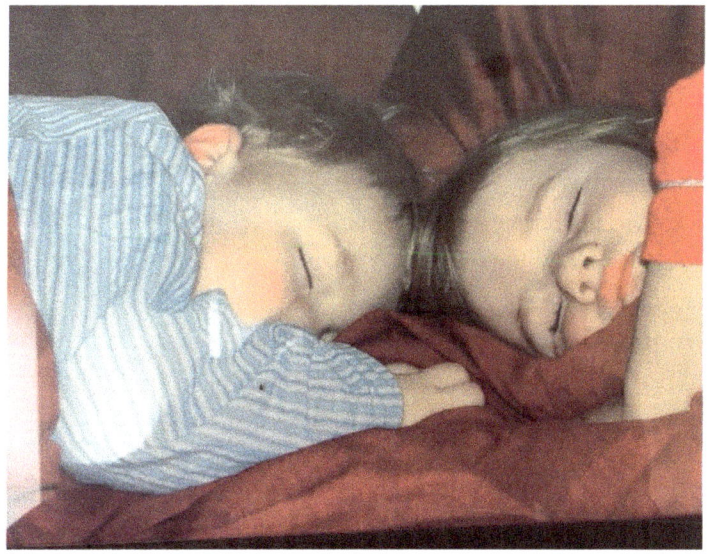

Wallpaper

Maybe it was too much to take on
Second time around.
Another rebuild top to bottom though not
Necessarily in that order.
Grade II listed was okay, done that before;
This time much more to do. New everything,
Taking single rooms separately, one at a time,
To live there in the big enough house.
We are family, two under three, one just a few months old.
It's what families do: build a home.
Though not always literally, physically, painfully.

So we toiled. Some done ourselves, most
With builders in and out, dust and dirt,
Brick and stone, plaster, and wood.
The bones of the building to hang the flesh upon,
Then make our own decorate paint and colour,
And wallpaper to smooth out imperfections.
It's an old house after all, and nothing is quite straight
Or even, or perfect;
And so we did build our home: literally, physically,
painfully.

It was worth it; a long slog with disagreements
Along the way, eventually done.
The bedrooms, loft conversion, new kitchen,
Colours chosen and applied inside and out.
Garden rearranged, clipped to perform,
Creating our idea of perfect: a landscape
To suit our ideal.
Not quite.
One room left, the living room, the main room,
The lounge where we should be together;
The last to be done remained undone.

That's how it remained through ill-health:
A time warp distinct from the rest of the house.
No fresh paint, curtains or shutters;
Bare floor requesting permanent comfort.
Everything in that one central place
Slowly decaying; no colour, no life, no wallpaper.

Last Night

Your feet were cold again as I rubbed them
To warm them in my hands.
You said they felt numb, so we walked
A few steps around the side ward.
To take the tingle away.

The antiseptic odour sticks in my nostrils
And in the back of my throat as we talk,
Soft whispers so not to disturb the snoozing
Line of others awaiting their time.

Nothing, in particular, is mentioned then you ask
What I am doing tomorrow.
"Taking the kids out with Jane and Jamie,"
I tell you as I look at your face, your eyes.

Then look away. The stark empty white walls
Change colour as I stare them out;
Shades of blue and orange and red and green
Alternate between the white and drift.

Big fluffy cumuli float across the ceilings and walls
To meet your voice somewhere in the back of my head.
What do I hear? "Sorry! Yes, I'm taking them out."
"Give them a big hug tonight.
Tell them I love them".

I nod and smile, and you mirror in your eyes and lips.

That was our last night.

First Day at School

Mum held your hand on your first day at school,
Carried your bag as you skipped to the gate;
Like ants from above, the kids won't be late.
This is the lesson, the very first rule.

When your turn came, it was dad's hand you held.
Was it different for you, was it strange?
You lined up with friends, unaware of the change,
Their minds and mouths busy, all else repelled.

Those school years are there for learning and fun,
But of real life, they don't tell you much.
No help at all; with a sensitive touch
Hurried you through, so you're all gone and done.

The happiest days of our lives, we're told,
Should help us grow as our futures unfold.

Three
Love me two times

Leaving

I am leaving now my little two,
But I will talk to you each day,
And listen to you when I do,
To hear what you have to say.

To Mum

I wanted to grow up with you
Smile, laugh, and cry.
To hold your hand, to run and jump.
I didn't want you to die.

You would have walked to school with me,
Watched as I waved goodbye.
Taken me to friends for tea.
I didn't want you to die.

And after school, we'd go to clubs
As you would watch me try,
To catch a ball and run around.
I didn't want you to die.

The chance to grow up with you here
Was taken without my
Knowing, awareness, or understanding.
I didn't want you to die.

Life's lottery rolls over for some,
Yours came too soon it seems.
Those few small things I do recall,
I cherish to fuel my dreams.

Heart Stones

I found these stones in the sand
Where we once strolled.
And chose each one to make a heart.
For you.

Blake's grains of sand outnumber by far
The flowers where you are.
And where we all will be.

These stones; too big to hide,
Too small to last forever,
Now washed away
With the tide.

All things must pass,
Fade away and disappear.
Gone in a moment,
No longer here.

Best Friend

I am here, waiting for you,
Your soul and what remains.
Pour into me your dust
And paraphernalia.

I am your resting place,
Your cubic centimetres of space.
A container to hold
All that you were.

Get to know me well;
We will be together for

a very

Long

Time.

Father's Hand (I)

Small boy holding dinner-plate hand,
Striding Daddy tugging along.

Old hand, paper-thin skin;
I want to rub it warm
But dare not.

A religious man but never assuming;
He knew God in his way,
His Father.

A talented scientist, Chemistry and Maths;
He knew everything when I knew nought.
"Zero is a man-made concept you know,
To help us mathematicians."
I didn't know what the hell he was talking about.

He met Mum on a bus on the way to a debate.
She was at art college, he at UMIST.
The bus was quite empty because in those days
Not all the population went to university.

So they talked.

We both feel the touch of skin.
Deliberately I draw my finger across its tissue paper-thin
And catch the smell of his breath as I lean towards him.
Hospital slow; the smell of death all around.

I remember when he wasn't looking;
I would sneak down and take a whiff.
He took a puff (snigger)
On his pipe.
I picked it up and held it in my palm. Looking around to check on my solitude,
I pretend to be Dad, a grown-up smoking pipe.

I still have his old tobacco tin
And see him when I open it and dip my nose in.
Sitting on his old leather chair holding a glass of single malt whiskey,
Whilst reading a book or testing me on my tables and spellings.

"Do you know Tchaikovsky? His music?"

Dad takes my hand as we walk together to the door,
Leading through past the hall to the room
Where we're not allowed anymore.

My heart beats faster. I wonder what
I'm about to see in the best room.
Dark floorboards, a huge Persian pattern rug.
A child-free Sanctuary.

In the corner, where a small box used to be,
Stands now a bigger box on narrow legs.
Different smells here now, leather and tobacco yes, but
mingled with wood
and hardly trod upon wool-weave.

Hand on my shoulder, he takes me over; my palms sweat
as he lifts the top,
Hinges pivoting it skywards revealing beneath:
A record player.

Speakers either side tilt forward mysteriously.
I watch, amazed at the magical mechanics
As Dad places his favourite violin concerto.
Wafting his conductor hands as the sound
Powers from this box of tricks.

As I listen to the sound, I look around at his shelves of
books.
And the piano in the corner where Grandma taught us to
play.
The books. Chemistry, Maths, History, and Religion.
Bibles and books about Bibles.
Sucking in the air with its presence, a huge leather-bound
Concordance.
Centre stage.

I would watch Dad take this tome from the shelf
And, as he opened the weighty covers,
The overpowering, throat-catching
Musty paper odours the room,

Filling the air with such intensity that my mum-made jumper
Retains the smell for days.
I'm not everybody's friend at school.

Old now, the box doesn't work, lost its magic.
Stopped spinning. Speakers unspoken.

I remember those smells of tobacco, leather, and spirit.
The Unholy Trinity.

He took my hand once, now I take His.

Rose

I chose this place as the poet
Carefully chooses words.
This was a gesture unspoken,
Written down now to be heard.

And as those words so deliberately picked,
I placed this rose to symbolise
Your life on earth
Fading. Not to glamourise

But to represent beauty.
The rock: solid, permanent.
A hard, unyielding feature
Cradles life briefly lent.

When I Grow Up

I am eight and when I grow up,
I will have my own house,
Be married and have children.
I will take care of my family
And keep working.

I WILL have a dog!

If I could have three wishes, I would:
One, go out to space
And visit the biggest star and
There, look back into the past.

I am six and when I grow up,
I will drink some beers at the pub
And have my own house.
When I'm forty, I will have a dog.

If I could have three wishes,
I would have a big poster of Ronaldo.

Louis

MY THREE WISHES FOR THE FUTURE

If I had three magical wishes for the future

My first wish would be ....

a big poster of Ronaldo playing football

My second wish would be ....

My third wish would be ....

Olivia

MY THREE WISHES FOR THE FUTURE

If I had three magical wishes for the future

My first wish would be ....

going out to space

My second wish would be ....

I'd like to se the biggest star on earth.

My third wish would be ....

To look back into past. (1970s and se the beatles.)

When I Was Three

I don't know your voice
Or have a memory
Of how you played with me
Or showed me how to hold
My spoon.

Tucked me up in bed.
Fed me.

I don't remember building a snowman
In the garden and chasing me with a fist of snow
In your hand to
Squash down the back of my neck.

I only know your face from the photos I have seen
And your sound from the videos Dad made
When we went out for the day or away on holiday.

Did we do that often?
I don't remember.

But what I do know is that you are part of me.
Woven into my fabric;
An inextricable, indivisible, inseparable link to my past.

You are me;
We are one.

Did I Say Goodbye?

When I kissed your lips
As you let out a sigh,
Did I turn and smile,
Did I say goodbye?

Alone at night,
Did you lay and cry?
Gaze at the moonlight
As time passed you by.

Looking back through life,
Asking yourself why
With a tear as you go,
As you wave goodbye.

Four
When the music's over

Daft Dad

Up early this morning, going out for the day,
The kids fast asleep still in bed.
Packed lunch to prepare to keep hunger at bay
Some time to sort out my head.

Cheese and ham sandwiches, crisps and pork pie;
Plenty of drinks are a must.
I know what they'll eat and what they might leave,
Myself, I'm not really fussed

Shorts, trunks and towels all packed in the bag;
Sun-cream and hats are there too.
Time now to wake them, breakfast is made,
Tea's in the pot left to brew.

"Come on kids, get up, it's time to get dressed,
Your cereal is ready to eat.
We're going to the seaside today don't forget!
Let's get going — we've traffic to beat."

They wolf down their cornflakes, dippy egg and toast,
Finish their tea and fresh juice.
And quick as a flash, they're at the front door
By the car, don't be late, no excuse.

"Woah! Hey! Come back here" I call.
"You've forgotten to brush your teeth!
Hurry now up the stairs, and mind you don't fall
Go steady, don't give any grief!"

Bags are all ready, packed lunch in the boot,
Then Louis comes down from upstairs.
An armful of toys, snorkel, and mask
Towels and trunks all in pairs!

"It's just for the day, we're not off for the week"
Daft Dad shouts out from the car.
"Now take them straight back, come down and get in,
We need to get going it's far!"

And so we arrive at the seaside by ten,
Find a spot by some rocks in the sand.
Lay out the towels, our bags, and a chair
Look a while at the lie of the land.

The kids strip off in their shorts and swimsuits
And run to the sea where it breaks.
Wade in, splash about, they're having such fun
I smile to see the freedom that awakes.

As they run and play, kick around in the sea,
Swim out deep then back for a splash.
So carefree and happy, children again
Their worries all gone in a flash.

I call them for drinks, "Are you hungry just yet?"
"Yes, we are, but we want fish and chips!"
So I head to the pier for "Award-Winning Food"
That'll put a few pounds on your hips!

"Look out for the seagulls; they're vicious you know,"
I warn them as they both tuck in.
"Hold them close to your chest; eat as quick as you can!
When you've finished, put your rubbish in the bin".

The sun's at its height, the heat starts to burn,
Take a rest from the beach for a stroll.
On the front for an ice-cream, the penny arcade
Play the hoops or shoot for a goal.

Walk back to the beach, our towels laid out
The sun casts a shadow that's long.
Watching the surfers, their boards as they flip
And swimmers incredibly strong.

I take out the packed lunch, the food we have left;
They both tuck in still hungry.
"There's sand in my sandwich." The name must be apt.
"We can't eat these!" the pair of them cry.

Getting late now, it's time to pack up;
It's been great fun but now we must go.
With our bags and our kit, we head off for the car,
Not goodbye but "adieu."

As I drive through the lanes, winding roads that I take,
They both fall asleep in the back.
And I think of the fun that they've had today
And the one thing I know they both lack.

At home now, we're there. Both silent and still,
Heads down, bodies a heap.
I carry them out, carefully and quietly,
Tuck them up in their beds still asleep.

The telly turned on, glass of wine in my hand;
A call, "Dad, we're hungry!!" I hear,
"There's sand in our pants, can we have a shower?
We'll be quick, you can still have a beer!"

So into the shower, quick rinse, and they're out;
On the mat, the talcum snow falls.
"Daft Dad" they both mock, then laugh as they run
Away from my "I'll get you!" calls.

"Read a story!" please, Dad. "Read a story!" they beg,
As they cuddle in closer to me.
I've hardly started the first page of the book,
And they're both fast asleep on my knee.

I lie there awhile enjoying this time,
Remembering the day we just had.
When my own snores awake me with a jolt and a start
Though not perfect, life isn't bad.

Every Day

I'm good at lists;
I make them every day.
Not just one, but many.
A list of lists you might say.

Things to do, things I should have done;
Jobs that are too late now.
Speaking out loud, cursing myself,
And the hours irreversibly gone.

When You were gone, I had no idea
What might lie ahead.
All the things I had to remember
Now that you were dead.

I'd always organised my thoughts,
A tick-box of what 'must-be' done;
Change that to 'should-be' as many
Remain incomplete. Not done.

That's one thing I wish I had known;
My lists would never be finished.
'Today' becomes tomorrow
As tasks are increased, not diminished.

Socks that start off as pairs
Mysteriously separate.
Nutritious meals I've prepared
Remain stubbornly on the plate.

My job — that was fun,
Rewarding, well-paid,
Becomes tiring and mundane,
Wearing and staid.

For all the things I thought I could do,
I could never do quite enough.
Piling up on the endless list,
An ever-growing mound of stuff.

I did not know our friends would un-friend,
Smile while turning away.
A path opens up as crowds dissipate
At school fetes, parties, and May Day.

If a hole could be dug to throw the tasks in,
I could jump in myself, hide as well.
The chores would all rot in the ground
Then no need to face my Hell.

But they're there when I wake the next day;
Everything goes back to the start.
And I'm cheered by the faces the children present;
Their eyes and their smiles warm my heart.

Chop, Chop

"I don't like carrots, Dad,
Don't like peas.
I hate cauliflower,
But I do like these!"

"Put those sweets down, Louis"
With a look says Dad.
"Come and help me,
And don't look sad.

'Cause you're not having those;
They're bad for your teeth.
Stand on this chair.
See — now you can reach!

With this little knife,
The celery you can chop
While I slice the mushrooms
And tomatoes from the shop.

They're all bought just now,
Healthy and fresh,
To help you grow strong
And run like the best.

These herbs I picked
From the garden today;
You can cut them all small
Then go out to play.

But before you do that,
Be careful! You're wobbling a bit!
We'll put it all in the pan,
Turn the heat on and cook it.

Come in now, it's ready.
You helped me make this;
It's spaghetti bolognese,
Your favourite dish."

Father's Hand (II)

A minute old, maybe two;
You look me up and down.
No focus yet, that will come,
As you screw your face to a frown.

You were late from the off, overdue;
They said you'd be here in due course.
Now you are, your hand safe in mine
And mine in yours.

I marvel at the tiny nail on the smallest finger,
A miniature perfectly formed.
The ticking hands slow time,
Listening to the quieting storm.

I met your mum in a pub,
An accident never planned.
Fate pointed a finger to a gap at the bar
So next to her I could stand.

It happened so fast, moving on, moving in;
All perfect, what more to give?
Then one came along and soon after, two;
New lives and a new life to live.

Is it in our hands, our future held?
Used wisely; hopes gained, fears dispelled.

Not so simple of course,
Though it seems at the time.
Are we ever in control, is anything planned?
The stars don't always align.

As your tiny hands grow, I am there
In the garden playing catch with a ball.
Digging holes, finding worms, planting bulbs for the spring
And carrying tools when I call.

I remember the time I was mowing the lawn;
You called and ran to my side.
"Hold tight!" I proclaimed as we walked up and down,
Then jumped in for a wheelbarrow ride.

Those half-size guitars I bought for you both,
You never quite got the hang.
Hearing you practice upstairs in your room,
A jumbled non-musical twang.

An outdoor games set, ball and bat,
Gloves so big both hands fit in one.
I hold the bat with you, take aim and swing,
Then like a missile, another one gone.

Confident now, you stand proud with poise;
The music kicks in from the band.
Your voice projects out to the crowd, tightly packed;
On the stage, you have total command.

With a group of young men, you stand at the crease,
Hit the ball back over his head.
The bowler looks up, hands on his hips
And wishes he was elsewhere instead.

Young adults both, your lives now begin
To take shape. Follow your heart.
As my father held my hand, I yours in turn,
You must decide on the next part.

Puddles

I wake before dawn in that hour
When darkness has a light,
A blueness that forces its way through
The blind, that keeps out the night.
And opens my eyes to the day.

Inside, I hear the wind blowing
Rain and sleet from outside
Against my window. Warning sign.
Meticulous planning awry,
Spring weather shows no place to hide.

Test the air outside, nostrils flared
Like horses; head held high.
The smell of rain, earthy and dank,
Invites me to shelter;
Teasing amid wetness or dry.

***

Two small people in the backseat
Safely tucked and strapped,
Bundles secured.

In front, one adult person, I sit.
Weave the car down winding lanes
To an open space where vehicles herd.

Our friends wave as we unbuckle,
Step out to greet them.
Two parents, two children

And dogs. Their dogs, lots of dogs.
Scrapping and barking and biting and sniffing,
In that most personal way.

The sky flits from light blue to grey;
The sun fights to brighten the day.
Clouds come and go, skud 'cross the sky;
Short showers fill puddles then die.

The dogs race ahead, a tumble of fur,
Divert from the path to the wood to find sticks to fight for.

The adults front and rear,
Sentries on watch guarding and guiding;
The children between.

***

The path slopes slowly down the valley.
Dotted randomly along the way,
Puddles.
Small ones in groups, or larger
Joined together in their singularity
inviting, calling, drawing in to play.

What are wellington boots for,
If not to jump and splash
Into puddles, one to another?
While parents' eyes roll and mouths gasp.

Too late, wet is wet.
Water and earth, two elements bound,
What forms they shape and yet
Short-lived, disappear in the ground.

Great fun and joy, free to run and play.
The landing thump forces a splish,
Splashing muddy water over and into boots,
Splodging sodden socks slipped inside.

***

A zig-zagging route from puddle to puddle
Makes conversation to baffle and befuddle.
Jumping and splashing from one to another,
The thoughts exchanged between sister and brother.

***

I like dogs, they are fun	(jump).
I wish we had one	(splash).
I want ham on my sandwich	(jump).
My feet are wet; I don't care	(jump).
Did Mummy have a dog?	(splash)
I hate cheese. And tomato	(jump)
Why did Mummy die?	(splash)
But you've got guinea pigs!	(splash)
Dad had a dog, why can't we?	(jump)
What is cancer?	(jump)
Guinea pigs are boring in their cage	(splash).
I think Dad did have a dog. And Mummy	(splash).
Did Dad bring crisps?	(jump)
That's why I want a dog	(splash).
Does everyone with cancer die?	(jump)
Freya is getting a dog!	(splash)
I didn't want Mummy to die	(stop);
Neither did I	(stop).

***

Running down to the bottom where
The puddles converge as a stream,
They sit with their friends on a bench,
Legs dangling down from the beam

Dog jumps up as a cheese sandwich flies
Through the air, well caught in her mouth.
She runs off protecting her prize;
Kids giggle while trying to hide.

***

I pretend not to notice.
The deed has been done,
And we must leave this place.
Hike another steep hill to get back
To the start.
The puddles have gone the way we return,
Remembered there to retrace.

Who Cares?

Hi, Mum. I'm sat up in bed coz I couldn't sleep, so I'm writing to you though Dad doesn't know so I will be very quiet. I can't put the light on or he might see so I've pulled my duvet up high over my face and put my phone on torch, so that I can see what I'm writing and then later, maybe tomorrow or when Dad isn't using the computer I will go to the study and sit at your desk to print it out well I'll have to type it first of course coz I'm writing this in the pad I got for Christmas.

I want to print it out coz I'm sending a photo I took of me on my phone and I'm being really silly pulling a face and sticking my tongue out and making a salute like I'm in the army but I'm not! Ha ha ha!

But you know <u>that</u> of course!

Today at school was cool I played with my best friend Elena (you remember, Elaine's daughter?) but now, she doesn't like her name! so she wants to be called El but her mum said NO and she can be Ella if she wants but I don't think she's gonna do that so I **am** calling her El coz she's my friend.

Mrs Cramp told me off for NO REASON today she said I was talking but I *wasn't*, not this time it's not always me! I hate her but she doesn't like me I know so who cares anyway?

I wish you could go and see Mrs Bender and tell her about Mrs Cramp, she really doesn't like me and she's always saying I'm useless at maths but I'm not I just don't understand it and when I say that she shouts, "WHY AREN'T YOU LISTENING? I'VE JUST EXPLAINED THAT" and I say "but you went too fast and could you say it again, please?"

But she carries on talking to someone else. I don't think she heard me.

Ssshhhh!

(Whispering) I think I heard Dad coming up the stairs so I'm gonna turn the phone light off now I'll finish my letter to you later. I'm gonna say a prayer for you now. I miss you soooooooo much.

Love You
Nite xxxxxxx

Letters You Did Not Write

You know what I wanted;
I had to look and look.
And dig in those places you used to live.
Empty the drawers and cupboards
In every nook.
Ah — the drawer I never saw
You open on any occasion. Maybe a special place
Where you could put precious things
That one day would show their face.

Not to me. They were not there.
But still I search,
In hope of finding your words written down.
Maybe the anticipation of finding is more exciting
Than discovery and what that might reveal.
Your thoughts, a paper clown.

Where did you hide them?
In your pockets, under the pillow, the bed,
Inside your desk in amongst your papers,
Maybe a book you recently read.
Nothing moved or touched; everything still in its place
Where you left them.
And left.

Did you think about those times?
The holidays we loved, first days at school?
You should tell me what to do. Where did you put that down?
I was your rock you told me; you, nobody's fool.

I never gave up you know, hoping.
That was my way; take a knock, get back up.
My way of coping.
But nothing.

So I told myself that was a good thing.
What if I did not want to know what you thought?
Did you see the future mapped?
As star-crossed lovers it was always going to happen
That way. You started but scrapped
Those scruffy handwritten notes you intended to expand
And leave for me to find.
Hidden, in my mind.

Those dark thoughts you had. I did not want to know
If you saw all that you would miss
But could not bring yourself to say
Or put down. Much better
A smile. A hug. A kiss.

The quest takes a rest
From the forensic archaeological scrapings.
My fingers worn, blisters on blisters
Scream to call it off.
"Leave it now; make your own story.
Write it yourself; that should be enough."

What is love in all its mystification?
The Selfish Gene has grown a conscience.
More than survival now, it's an attempt — an effort to
redeem itself.
To turn basic instinct into something more profound;
We feel the loss and the friend we weep for.
Turning back would be just as hard and so
We go over.

Not giving up completely, the gaps between my mission
Widen. Days into weeks into months.

Stopped searching, I am halted in my mundanity
As there it is. The letter I have emptied pockets for,
Sofas, cupboards and drawers.
Have you emptied your heart, released your thoughts
Onto a blank white sheet to offer all yours?
All you have.

If I could fall from the greatest height,
Cliff dive into the most dangerous waters,
Leap from space without a parachute;
I thought I could not face a greater let down.

Not an ode of Shakespearian magnificent fate
But an old reminder of things we needed to do;
A list of priorities and 'to be done by' dates
To complete the renovation.

My heart at once sinks then rises.
I am glad.
I smile at remembering things we did together,
Bickering about the house paint colour, then,
Hundreds of samples on the back wall.
Probably only ten!

I never find a letter, a note, even a scribble
On an old supermarket receipt pencilled across.
Stop wondering if one night late,
You did put pen to paper then tear it up,
Not tempting fate.

Those letters you did not write are not important now.
A way for me to file away what might have been,
What had been left behind, and is,
Yet to come.

Dad Day

Wake them at seven, they're still half asleep
Breakfast laid out, the toast it'll keep.
Tidy away, make up the bed
Upstairs to get dressed, now they're all fed.
Put washing in, walk up to school
Straight off to work, no time to fool.
Drive to a meeting, maybe the train
Colleagues and clients all sound the same.
Write a report, respond to a note
Then back in the car and forget all I spoke.
Take a phone call speeding along
Turn on the radio, they're playing our song.
The news breaks the sound, all doom, and gloom
Kids to pick up, be home soon.
After school club football tonight
A quick pasta meal should be all right.
Before heading to brownies, wait in the car
While doing his homework, good job it's not far.
Straight back home, it's now getting late
Quick wash and brush, into bed by eight.
Never make that one though always the plan!
We all try our best, do what we can
Storytime now, a book that's been read
From cover to cover stuck in my head.

Nearly asleep, downstairs to wash up
Tidy the kitchen then pour a cup.
Check my emails work for next day
When it all starts again, and again,

That's the way.

(Homage to "Woman Work" by Maya Angelou)

Waving?

I felt the noose tight
Around my neck. My breathing
Slowed, gave in the fight.

Five
People are Strange

Kids Are Horrible Part 1
Ring O' Roses

Livvy's got no Mummy
She didn't come from her tummy
She went to bed
And woke up dead
We all think that's funny.

Ha fucking ha.

Kids Are Horrible Part 2
Playtime

The playground is a dangerous place
For any game
Fair Game
        (Play fair)

The boys boot a football, hard smack in the face
One down
How many more green bottles?
Take aim.
Another one down
Fair game
        (Play fair)

Girls in a corner whisper and plot
"You're it" they all shout and point
To the one with snot
Popping in and out as she breathes hard
To catch someone.
        (Play fair)
Fight!

The kids know where to go and swarm
Like bees around arms and legs,

Flailing. Windmills in a storm.
One pulls hair and the other one begs.
   (Play fair)

Teachers too slow, still drinking his tea
And dunking the biscuit the goody girl brings
Not noticed what's happened and then the bell rings.

Stand still
Line up.
"Did you enjoy playtime?"
   (Play fair)

Kids Are Horrible Part 3
Time Heals

Would you know me if you saw me now,
And would you still like me?

The Gardener

I love my garden. The battles, the imperfections, the bond it promotes, and the beauty it provides. It has always been a place to take me out of the everyday, to dirty my hands, sweat my brow, dig on cold winter days, deadhead on late summer evenings after I return from hours sat in an office, in a car or on a train.

There is a tree I planted, a Japanese Acer, planted in a corner, protected from strong winds, its red leaves transparent in the sunlight cast a shimmering shadow dappled on the ground below. I have watched it grow; each autumn, as it drops those ruby leaves, I thoughtfully prune the branches to form the most aesthetic shape, pleasing on the eye. Turning full circle, I am content with what I see, what I have done, and how the garden has followed nature with prudent taming here and there.

In another corner, further round in fuller sun, there is a rose that troubles me. For it is not well. For the first twelve years, it has blossomed, each summer grown bigger and stronger, an abundance of scented pink blooms that announce the arrival of each summer, and there they stay through the long daylight hours. One flower dies, pollinated by the bees that make busy around those floral stems, then three more burst into colour bringing life and light to the early autumn shorter days.

This year, its 13th, the leaves are brown, mottled with a colour that taunts the usually deep shiny green; an infection that eats away at its very heart, an invisible worm feeding in the night. The roots pull something from the deep below reflecting in its health above. Perhaps I have not fed it so well, or prepared the ground with sufficient nutrition, not giving the roots enough strength to burrow down deep and support itself for those summer months taking elements from the earth as vines do, giving life to its fruits; the terroir in which the plant derives its unique character announcing, stating, confirming, 'This is who I am, this is where I'm from.'

I thought it was strong enough needing less care, but my rose begins to wither, the buds that flower sag, weeping for itself; the wind whispers, "Give up, you've done your time." Who fed my rose that I do not know of? What causes harm?

I am the gardener, so I must not give up. I must try all I know, not turn my back on my rose that gave so much joy before. This challenge is my focus above all others. The thorns seem sharper now, many more that aim their needle points at my hand as I reach out to nurture. Angry with me they prick and stab, and I bleed. But blood dries up, and I can protect myself with gloves and thicker clothes. So I cover up, toughen up.

I seek out help, a friend, a local elder wiser sage, an expert and another and another as this is now beyond my ken; no books provide the answer. I need these eyes to cast upon the affliction and give up their advice, their time, their salvation; their varied remedies tried or otherwise.

The seasons pass; my rose survives but is in a poor way. I have sheltered and fed it with manure, bone meal, blood (my blood!). I have carefully tended each season as I should and those that know have all looked and offered their opinion. But it is down to me. I dig the ground in which it sits and draws life. I make a bigger hole and move it to a place that might be better, a wall behind that reflects the heat. I try all I can and all that I am told.

I am stubborn to persist with this cause, determined to succeed, but this single plant means more than anything, and I cannot let it die. Its survival and return to health consume my waking thoughts and overtakes my sleeping hours. More seasons pass, years fade, and I feed, tend and nurture my rose. There are some blooms, and they are as beautiful as ever but not as bountiful. Digging and pruning, feeding and weeding, taking out the weaker stems, removing the diseased parts to encourage the healthy, my rose, eventually, at last, begins to grow stronger.

In its 18th year, it is in full bloom. The summer is here, and it is warm — some days even hot! Each day when it does not rain, I water my rose; each week I feed it, I have fed the soil and so the roots have remained strong, grounded in fertile earth. The flowers fulsome and pink that blush in the warm summer evenings and send a scent signal to the busy bees that gather around, bustling one another out of the way to be the first to the nectar they seek out from the blooms that signal their good health.

Haiku

For twelve years, it grew.
My rose; the blossoms flowered,
Then struggled to live.

Horticulturists
Did all they could to help it
Recover and shine.

Years came, and years went.
From poor health, my rose grew strong.
A fine example.

Extra Time

My heart is blown, bigger than a football,
Waiting to burst.
Kick me hard, so I can kick you
And get sent off, banned for life, forgotten.

The commentator talks about the game of two halves.
I just want to play in the first half
When we are winning;
Team talk before they all come out again,
And it's a different game.
Who's losing now?

Is it about life and death
Or more important than that?
If I play no more then I can forget,
And you will tell me to retire.
All over now, find something new.

Try a different game perhaps;
Keep walking, keep walking, don't look back
Keep walking.

I'm tired now, breathing deep;
They bring on the substitute.

My bones are old,
My flesh withered,
My blood runs thin,
My eyes are dull,
My ears not sharp.

I want to walk with you
Down the tunnel to the dressing room
Where we never change, never return.

No comeback game
No extra time.

Hymn to Whoever

All things bright and beautiful, it says you made them all.
Were you watching as I faded?
Waiting for the fall.

Young girl sings the words at school
Loud voice with faith and cheer.
Rousing and raising together as one
Innocent children we hear.

I lie awake.
The only sound the beating of my heart
For a moment I think I can hear blood
Moving
Through my body.

Did it stop?
Slow down?
My hands together I pray
Cold feet warming at his touch
Lay your hands and raise me up.

What will I tell them when I'm gone?
Death is easy for us who die
Much harder for those left to lie
Alone. Awake and thinking
Drifting, floating. Sinking.

Are you listening to my lament?
Telling yourself my chances spent.
What right have you to take away
My life, my loves, and future days?

I bang my head and fist the wall
I know you haven't heard me, ignored my call.
Was I bad, did something wrong,
That forces you to forsake me in MY hour of need?

Not forgiven.

Each surviving day is written as a triumph
But tomorrow brings another waiting game.
Leave me dangling, hanging
Each breath, one closer 'til you call my name.

You're not there, are you?
That's why you don't reply.
Any sign would do but none come back,
And so I wait to die.

How to solve this universal mystery?
The question asked since thinking began.
Where do we come from and more,
Where do we go?

Have we not always sought to know
The answer that is never given?
And at the end, we turn,
Relent, repent, seek forgiveness
From our sins. In hope

The Lord giveth,
And the Lord taketh away.
Matter cannot be created or destroyed
Nothing becomes nothing, black is white is grey.

I go on for now and not eternity,
As I was born and die,
So I gave life to thee.

All things bright and beautiful
Fade away and die
All things must pass not stay,
That you made them is a lie.

Be Kind

Don't hurt me with your cruel words
Photos and messages to hide behind.

Be thoughtful and honest to yourself
But most of all,

To others, be kind.

my good health

i have a box that helps me
 when i'm sad.
inside are different plasters labelled
'sad', 'head-hurt', 'unusual'

a small tin for my cuddle potion
that dad gives me every night

two medicine bottles one which is for
head injuries, weak bones, and sadness

and another that is a listening bottle
so I can hear the voice of my mum

that one is empty.

Why?

What made you so evil
That you chose to try and destroy
The people you had left, the ones
You should love most?

I was strong, able to resist
Your moves, your attempts to slur
And stain. Besmirch me to those
Who had to listen,

So they did. Lawyers, Police, Social Services,
Teachers, Judges, neighbours,
My family and friends.

You made me suffer again and again,
Reveal my pain to all made to listen.
Your tenacity was commendable but would be better served
In some other way.

Now after all those years,
You come again. The same nasty
Snide remarks
Designed to burn, hurt, scar.

Skip a generation, try it on
The younger ones. But they see through you.
Your grandchildren see what you are too.

I Can't Say How You Should Feel

Dave offered me a pint of bitter or
Maybe I'd prefer a whiskey. At the
Bar, small crowd gathered 'round to offer him
Condolences. With an unspoken look

Some presented a hand to shake or pat
On the shoulder, not too affectionate.
The men: mostly in dark suits and black ties
A few years unworn and a few years tight.

Dave looked at me, opened his mouth to speak
Then has to turn to take another kiss
On the cheek, a hug, a tap on the back
And more quiet heartfelt words for his loss.

A chance now, a lull as light bites arrive
The words came out, stuttering whisky slow.
"You understand how it is," he says, but
I say, "Dave, I can't say how you should feel.

It's different for both of us you see
The pain, the hole, all of the loss is real.
We each have to find our own way to deal
With sadness. I can't say how you should feel."

Hit the Ground Running

It's all online now the job-seeking lark
Anonymous decisions hiding behind
A form to fill in.

We're an ambitious employer looking for
Talent and energy, positive words
Dotted everywhere, thrown up in the air
To land on every page.

"Diverse, Growth, Entrepreneurial and Collaborative
Dynamic, Determined, Individuals with Drive."

We are all of these, and we want you to be the same.

If we don't give you an interview
Too busy for feedback, you're in the 'NO' pile.
There's no one to call and ask why
We've word-searched your papers, you don't fit the profile.

Don't give up, keep trying. I'm sure you'll get something
Before you're really old.
Meantime, your skills fade and disappear,
And you've been left out in the cold.

Six
My eyes have seen you

First Date

It's a feeling I've not had for many years
The anticipation, the quickening heartbeat
The thoughts in my head, some of them fears
Amplification of sounds, echoes in the street.

I hesitate to be the first to go in
So I stand in the courtyard and wait.
That makes me more nervous, so I look around
At the old-wall building and wrought iron gate.

Footsteps bounce down the narrow passageway
Sounding louder and closer. They collide,
Mingling with the seconds earlier steps, they
Must be more than one person's stride.

Tick. Ba-bump. Tock. Ba-bump.

You smile as you see me but with a considered look,
I notice your hair and jewellery neat,
A petrol blue dress leads down
To the thin-strapped silver sandals on your feet.

From the passage into a cobbled courtyard
Tables and chairs dotted freely; good choice!
Up two shallow steps through glass doors we stroll
And meet a girl at a desk with a confident voice.

The glass and the marble, pristine chat in a well-mannered clip
Waiters crisp white and black.
We are led to our place, formally laid out
Beside a bare stone wall at the back.

At the table, we talk about dating sites
That it seems to be the only way to meet
New people, a change from the usual group.
Who goes to discos now, and pubs are so loud you can't speak.

Each course that arrives brings a fresh conversation
Awkward at first, but food is a good icebreaker.
Who can cook, what we like, our favourite place,
Italian, French, fish, chicken, or steak.

Yes, all of those and more we concur!
(Which I'm glad about, you might think I'm a greed!)
Nervous talk at first now chattering free
Like the rest of the tables, an unnoticed sepia bleed.

After lunch, we walk together through the town
A few minutes to the bus, then goodbye on our way.
We turn, a cheek kiss and plan to meet again,
Another time, another place, another day.

How different from my very first date.

We had met before in the store where I worked
On a Saturday. You came in, smiling and tall.
I worked on the music counter, and it was quiet
So you chose a record to play I recall.

After a few visits like that (a drawn-out affair)
You invited me for a meal. With your mum and dad.
I accepted of course though not what I had in mind.
You told your parents, I thought I was mad!

I had no choice or say in the matter
They knew a new venue they called a Berni Inn.
I arrived early to impress, a long way from home
In Didsbury, a posh suburb where they drank wine and gin.

This was all new and strange to me, a young kid
Standing outside this huge white-painted facade.
The wait torturing my lungs and laughing at me
As I grew evermore anxious. Scarred

I thought, forever if they didn't arrive.
They did. Friendly and welcoming.
You stood there, slightly back
Neither of us knowing quite what to do, your parents hovering.

The double door entrance, large hinges, and studs
Made to look like a medieval clink.
Inside a swarm of waiters buzzing 'round tables
A long bar, more waiters, waiting to collect food and drink.

'70s luxury. The height of posh taste, we are led
To our place neatly set out, plain and smart.
The girls sit with backs to the wall men face,
Knives and forks ready, condiments like soldiers ready to start.

The menu so simple, chicken or steak with chips
And a bottle, you choose: red or white?
Your dad has spoken, decided, job done
As we all settle down for a marvellous night.

The waiter comes over and lights a candle
Stuck on a bottle covered in dripping wax.
No ordinary bottle, this one's from Spain
Half-covered in raffia, exotic and foreign. Nothing plain

About tonight. A gathering still remembered.
A place stuck in Tardis Time carried along with fate.
My first real girlfriend, her parents, and me.
I wonder if she recalls our first date.

In Blood

Throw the dice,
Lead me on this unchosen path
That I did not foresee,
Not want.

What do I do now?
What course left but two?
To carry on or give in
Neither seeming preferable than one.

When winds prevail and blow in storms
When lightning strikes nearby.
When rains fall heavy and soak,
Do we run away?

We hide, take cover, and wait for passing.
And when the sun returns,
Rejoice, take pleasure
In the warmth it bestows.

Gardens

What are gardens but manicured, manipulated
Square metres of nature tamed.
We love our gardens, I love my garden!
The immediacy of a lawn's freshly mown stripes,
The smell of cut grass in summer.
Autumn leaves raked into piles
For the compost; food for the earth.

A garden is a physical symbol of future hope
Regrowth, rebirth, reincarnation.
The Hanging Gardens of Babylon
The Garden of Eden, Gethsemane;
Myths and legends, religious tales
Tell the truth of the cycle of life.
High praise for high ideas to nurture
Nature for our physical and
Emotional wellbeing.

The seasons. From one year to the next,
Life emerges, dies, and comes again.
Winter clipping pays off in spring
As green shoots first appear
Then flourish as daylight hours extend
And sunshine warms the earth.

Water, the key to life, unlocks the dry
Touching microscopic roots, quenching the urge
To burst into flower (as nuggets of nutrition
From stores below), then raise their heads to nod.

rearviewmirror 16/4

I saw you in my rearviewmirror
Reflected back behind

You stood still, fixed in that moment
As I moved forward in automatic

My self-charging automobile gathered pace
Along the road, relatively speaking

Where did those years go? The passage of time
Is a strange thing seemingly standing still

Then speeding up as we grow further apart
I saw you in my rearviewmirror

Then you were lost to the distance
Still there, yet gone.

Let Go

Of course it's hard
Make no mistake.
Each day like the last
And the next, without break.

A relentless Catherine Wheel
Of pain,
That gradually slows as it turns
Again

And again, until suddenly one day
It stopped.

And you know
You have let go.

Snowflake

My children's generation have been called snowflakes
No stamina or concentration.
When life gets hot they disappear
Lacking will and determination.

Yet snowflakes are beautiful
Pure and unique, no one like any other.
Look closely and see
How they form a perfect symmetry

As they individually fall from above
They join to become one
Wondrous Winterland of White
United in what they have become.

Together a stronger singularity
Covering imperfection
Showing a perfect view
A new world they have created.

Theirs is the future, not ours
A bright beginning to behold.
As they melt they bring new life
A brilliance to unfold.

Three Things You Should Know

you are stronger than you think.

no one can tell you how you should feel.

you are vital and your experiences worthy of sharing.

How Far You've Come

Dad
Are you watching now, keeping track?
Perhaps you keep a record
Every day a new fact.

By the bed where you lie,
Pick up and write
With pencil or pen as you see us.
Day and night.

Mum
He's been a good boy today
Homework all done.
Hurry up, get ready there's rugby to play
Watching, smiling at your fun.

Hospital visit, hope you're better soon!
I could reach down and stroke your hair,
Ease your pain from midnight to noon
Protecting, your troubles laid bare.

My pages are ragged, well-thumbed and torn
As I flick through the years.
Turn the leaves back and forth; I can mourn
As you cry. But I shed no tears.

My diary starts from the day I left.
I copied the words that you wrote
On the card with the flowers, I saw
Your infant scrawl, your note.

Not one can say
That they understand.

Though I did.

No more tomorrows for me now
But I keep writing. It helps me remember
So I can look back, someday
To show you where you've been,
How far you've come.

Dad
It's only a dream I keep telling myself,
You smile at me back in reply
Moments to cherish, forever hold close
Explanations that don't answer why.

Turn the lights out, lie down in the dark
Hear the silence that wraps around.
Though we try to close the infinite space
Our emptiness is still, light and sound.

Mum
That first Christmas I wrote and wrote.
And noted you open neatly wrapped gifts,
Pondered how soon it's forgotten
As you played out your childish tiffs.

Of course, I know you haven't.
It's Christmas, you're happy and pleased
Running around the house eating chocolate and sweets
Your faces alight at the toys you've received.

Summer the third year, all ready and packed
Dad tells you to hurry, can't be late.
Organising movements, a motherly act
Queuing up for your flight by the gate.

On the beach, in the sea, your laughter observed
Fish and chips, the penny arcade.
The seagulls that gather not waiting for scraps
Make sandcastles and watch the light fade.

Dad's big birthday, all out for a meal
I think he might have one or two!
The smile on his face as you sing him a song
The eyes that tell me what's true.

The years skip by and my pages fill.
I've seen you all of the while.
At school,
With your friends,
Drama, music, and sports
Young adults with your own style.

No more tomorrows for me now
But I keep writing. It helps me remember
So I can look back, someday
To show you where you've been and,
How far you've come.

www.ingramcontent.com/pod-product-compliance
Lightning Source LLC
LaVergne TN
LVHW021948060526
838200LV00043B/1955